First Simple Recipes for Little Kids and Adults

By Sarah Mason

Copyright ©2020 by Sarah Mason

All rights reserved. Printed in the United States of America. No part of this book may be used or reproduced in any manner whatsoever without written permission except in the case of brief quotations embodied in critical articles and reviews.

For more information please contact at simplerecipecookbooks@gmail.com.

ISBN: 978-0-578-75405-5

Contents

Introduction	7
Starters	9
Mains	13
Sides	21
Desserts	25

Introduction

Healthy eating is important at all ages. Moderation and portions are important. From experience, asking what my child should eat never came back with a good answer. What we feed children uses portions smaller than for an adult according to professional guidance. Over time, I have found recipes that are scalable to small eaters and big eater that all ages enjoy.

These easy recipes are simple and can be changed by adding dips or sauces. This book includes starters, mains, sides, and desserts. Try a combination for a simple mealtime for any day of the week.

Starters

Tomato Salad

Ingredients
1 pint grape tomato medley
¼ tsp salt
1/8 tsp black pepper

Directions
Wash grape tomatoes under water and dry
Cut each grape tomato in half
Place tomatoes in bowl
Sprinkle tomatoes with salt and pepper

Color Stix

Ingredients
2 small Kirby cucumbers
1 medium red pepper
3 medium carrots

Directions
Wash cucumbers, carrots, and red pepper under water
Peel carrots and cut off ends
Peel cucumbers and cut off ends
Cut top off red pepper and remove seeds inside
Cut cucumber, carrot, and red pepper in strips
Arrange the bright vegetable stix on a plate

Beef and Vegetable Soup

Ingredients
1 ½ lbs. beef stew meat
1c corn or potato starch
1 large onion
4 medium carrots
2 celery stalks
1 14oz can of petite diced tomato
3 medium potatoes
1 ½ c frozen green beans
2 beef bouillon cubes
1 tsp garlic powder
½ tsp dried thyme
½ tbs salt
½ tsp black pepper
4c water

Directions
Remove skin from onion and cut into small pieces
Peel and cut carrots into ½ in rounds
Place corn or potato starch on a plate and dredge the stew meat in the starch
Place all ingredients into a pot
Cook covered on medium heat for 1 hour

Mains

Oven Fried Chicken

Ingredients
1 chicken cut into pieces, I prefer eights
2 tbs Olive oil
Olive oil cooking spray
¾ c Mayonnaise
1c Gluten free pancake mix
1 ½ Corn flake crumbs
1 tsp sugar
1 tsp salt
½ tsp black pepper
1 ½ tsp sweet paprika
2 one gallon food bags

Directions
Rinse chicken pieces with water
Place mayonnaise into a gallon plastic bag
Place all dry ingredients into a gallon plastic bag
Take chicken pieces one at a time, place into mayonnaise bag to coat, then the dry ingredient bag to coat
Place coated chicken piece in pan

Repeat until all chicken pieces in pan
Pour olive oil into pan in between pieces of chicken
Spray chicken with cooking spray
Place pan uncovered in oven at 350 for 1 hour 25 minutes

Grilled Chicken

Ingredients

2 large boneless chicken breasts cut in half
1 tsp baking soda
2 c water
1 tbs soy or gluten free soy sauce
½ c barbeque sauce
1 tbs honey
1 tsp garlic
1 gallon food bag

Directions

Place chicken in bowl with water and baking soda. Stir frequently and wait 15 minutes
Take chicken out of bowl, rinse, and dry
Take all remaining ingredients in bag
Place bag with chicken into fridge for 4 hours, turning the chicken in bag several times
Remove chicken from bag
Place chicken on hot grill pan turning Once to cook evenly

Giant Meatballs

Ingredients

1 ½ lbs. mixed ground meat
1 egg, lightly beaten
½ c cornflake crumbs
1tsp garlic powder
1tsp salt
½ tsp black pepper
2 tbs dried parsley flakes
Canola oil spray

Directions

In a large bowl, mix meat, egg, cornflake crumbs, garlic powder, salt, pepper, parsley flakes
Spray canola oil on a large baking sheet
Divide mixture to make 12 balls
Place balls on baking sheet and spray with canola oil
Cook in 400 oven for 45 minutes

The "Original" Taco

Ingredients

1 lb. of ground beef
1 14 oz can refried beans
1 packet taco seasoning
¼ c water
12 tortillas, hard or soft taco sized
2 plum tomatoes (Optional)
Shredded lettuce (Optional)
Packaged guacamole (Optional)

Directions

Cook ground beef in pan on medium heat until browned in small pieces
Add taco seasoning and ¼ c water, simmer 5 minutes on low heat
Warm refried beans in a pan on stove for 5 minutes
Cut tomatoes into small pieces
Serve combination of meat, beans, tomatoes, lettuce, and guacamole in each shell

Meaty Fried Rice

Ingredients

1c Cooked shredded steak
2c Cooked rice
½ c Peas
1 tsp sugar
2 tbs Sesame oil
1 tsp Ground ginger
2 tbs Soy Sauce

Directions

Add oil to a hot pan on stove
Add cooked steak and rice, peas, sugar, ginger, and soy sauce
Stir frequently until ingredients are hot and mixed

Sides

Broccoli
Ingredients: Broccoli, 2c water
Directions: Wash and place chopped broccoli in a covered pot with 2c water on medium heat for 15 minutes

Sautéed Cabbage
Ingredients: 3c cabbage, ½ c olive oil, 1 tsp sugar, salt, and pepper
Directions: Take chopped or shredded cabbage place in a pan with ½ c olive oil, salt, pepper, and 1 tsp sugar. Cook on medium heat stirring cabbage frequently until soft

Roasted Vegetables
Ingredients: 1lb. carrots, 1 lb. parsnips, 1 yellow pepper, 1 red pepper, oil, salt, pepper
Directions: Peel and cut carrots, parsnips into chunks. Remove seeds from a yellow and a red pepper, slice each into thin strips. Take vegetables and mix in bowl with oil, salt, and pepper. Place on a baking sheet in oven at 450 for 30 minutes

Garlic Potato Mash

Ingredients: 4 medium russet potatoes, 1 tsp garlic powder, salt, and oil

Directions: Take 4 medium russet potatoes, wash and cut into chunks. Place in a pot, cover with water. Cook over medium heat for 30 minutes. Drain. Add 2 tsp salt, 1 tsp garlic powder, and 1 tbs oil. Blend with a hand blender in batches or use a food processor on low speed to mash potatoes into a smooth texture

Rice

Ingredients: 1c long grain rice, 2c water

Directions: Place 1c rice in a pan. Add 2c water to 9x9 pan. Cover and place on 350 in oven for 1 ½ hours

Desserts

Fruit Mix

Ingredients

1c dried cranberries

1c dried pineapple chunks

½ c chocolate chips

Directions

Mix ingredients in a large bowl

Brownies

Ingredients

1 ½ c all-purpose flour or gluten free blend
1c granulated sugar
1 egg
¾ c oil
½ tsp vanilla extract
½ c cocoa powder
¾ tsp baking powder
¼ c water
½ c chocolate chips

Directions

In a large bowl, mix all wet ingredients
Add sugar to wet ingredients and stir to combine
Add flour, cocoa, and baking powder. Stir until smooth
Add chocolate chips. Mix well
Pour into an 8x8 pan and bake 50 min at 350

Blondies

Ingredients

1 ½ c all-purpose flour or gluten free blend
1c granulated sugar
1 egg
¾ c oil
1 tsp vanilla extract
¾ tsp baking powder
¼ c water
½ c chocolate chips (Optional)
½ c caramel chips (Optional)

Directions

In a large bowl, mix all wet ingredients
Add sugar to wet ingredients and stir to combine
Add flour and baking powder. Stir until smooth
Add in chocolate chips and caramel chips. Mix well
Pour into an 8x8 pan and bake 50 min at 350

Candy Popcorn

Ingredients

2c popped white popcorn

Popcorn salt

Canola oil

8 oz baking chocolate

Directions

Place popcorn in a bowl and drizzle with oil

Sprinkle salt to taste on popcorn in bowl and stir to mix

In a microwave, heat the chocolate in a bowl until melted and smooth

Pour popcorn into a deep roasting pan lined with parchment paper

Drizzle half the chocolate over the popcorn and stir

Drizzle second half of chocolate over popcorn and stir

Let cool for 1 hour

Birthday Cake

Ingredients

1 ¾ c all-purpose flour or gluten free blend
¾ c white sugar
3 eggs
½ c oil
¾ c rice or soy milk
1 ¼ tsp vanilla extract
½ tsp baking soda
¾ tsp baking powder
¼ c colored sprinkles (Optional)
1 can vanilla frosting (Optional)

Directions

In a large bowl, mix all wet ingredients
Add sugar to wet ingredients and stir to combine
Add flour, baking powder and baking soda. Stir until smooth
Add sprinkle and mix well
Pour into an 8x8 pan
Bake 50 min at 350
Let cool for 3-4 hours. Spread top with vanilla frosting

www.ingramcontent.com/pod-product-compliance
Lightning Source LLC
Chambersburg PA
CBHW061316040426
42444CB00010B/2674